Getting Around with Dogs

By Jordan Avery

People love patting dogs!

But working dogs should not be patted!

Dogs can learn lots of jobs, like getting something off the ground.

If someone can't see well, they can walk around by tapping and dragging a cane from side to side.

If the cane hits something, it is letting the person know to stop.

But canes can't tell someone that it is not safe to cross a road.

A dog won't let someone cross until the cars have stopped.

By sitting still, dogs tell people that it is not safe to cross.

Until 1928, people who could not see well only had canes to help them get around.
Then Mr Frank's dog, Buddy, learned to help!

Mr Frank was blind, and he planned to show that Buddy could keep him safe.

Mr Frank stepped onto a street crossing, and Buddy led him to the other side!

TAXI

Dogs help people with lots of things.

This dog's job is sitting with and getting patted by sick people.

It is okay to pat this dog!

This man was sadder before patting the dog!

This dog's job is stopping people from falling.

If a puppy does something again and again, that thing turns into a habit.

It learns things like walking without running, stopping at crossings and grabbing things for people.

When the puppy gets bigger, it starts to work.

When work is finished, dogs can be hugged.

That is the biggest prize for a working dog!

CHECKING FOR MEANING

1. How do dogs tell people it's not safe to cross a road? *(Literal)*
2. What are three things dogs do to help people? *(Literal)*
3. Why should you not pat some dogs? *(Inferential)*
4. How do you think people feel about their helper dogs? Why? *(Evaluative)*

EXTENDING VOCABULARY

dragging	What is the base of the word *dragging*? How does adding the suffix *ing* to *drag* change the meaning? What does it mean to drag something?
planned	What is the base of the word *planned*? How does adding the suffix *ed* to *plan* change the meaning?
bigger	What is the base of the word *bigger*? How does adding the suffix *er* to *big* change the meaning?

MOVING BEYOND THE TEXT

1. Dogs can do many things for us. What other jobs can dogs do?
2. What other animals can be trained to help people?
3. What might happen if you touch a puppy while it is training?
4. Have you ever trained a dog to do a trick or do something useful for you? What did you teach it, or what would you like to teach a dog?

TIME TO WRITE

Write about something a dog could do to help you.